D0296201

CAERPHILLY COUNTY BOROUGH

Tynnwyd o'r stoc
Withdrawn

To my mother, Gerri, for her endless love

CAERPHILLY COUNTY BOROUGH COUNCIL	
3 8030 08122 4613	
ASKEWS & HOLT	31-Jan-2012
J599.759	£10.99
LIB0755	

JANETTA OTTER-BARRY BOOKS

Eye on the Wild: Cheetah copyright © Frances Lincoln Limited 2012
Text and photographs copyright © Suzi Eszterhas 2012

The right of Suzi Eszterhas to be identified as the author and photographer of this work
has been asserted by her in accordance with the Copyright, Designs and Patents Act,
1988 (United Kingdom).

First published in Great Britain in 2012 by
Frances Lincoln Children's Books, 4 Torriano Mews,
Torriano Avenue, London NW5 2RZ
www.franceslincoln.com

All rights reserved

No part of this publication may be reproduced, stored in a retrieval system, or transmitted,
in any form, or by any means, electrical, mechanical, photocopying, recording or otherwise
without the prior written permission of the publisher or a licence permitting restricted copying.
In the United Kingdom such licences are issued by the Copyright Licensing Agency,
Saffron House, 6-10 Kirby Street, London EC1N 8TS.

A catalogue record for this book is available from the British Library.

ISBN 978-1-84780-204-0

Set in Stempel Schneidler

Printed in Dongguan, Guangdong, China by Toppan Leefung in November 2011

1 3 5 7 9 8 6 4 2

CHEETAH

Suzi Eszterhas

F

FRANCES LINCOLN
CHILDREN'S BOOKS

Far away, on the plains of Africa, baby cheetahs are born. They are called cubs. There are usually six to eight brothers and sisters in a cheetah family, and they love snuggling up next to Mum to keep warm.

Cheetah cubs are helpless and blind when they are first born, with their eyes and ears firmly closed. When they are hungry, they make a noise that sounds like a baby bird chirping. This is why a cheetah's den is called a 'nest'.

Cheetah cubs are always hungry. They need to drink a lot of their mother's milk so they will grow big and strong. Sometimes, when Mum is away hunting, they don't drink for almost the whole day – and then they get really hungry! The cubs drink milk every day, until they are three months old.

By the time the cubs are ten days old, they have grown much bigger. Their eyes and ears have opened and they can walk pretty well, but Mum still makes them stay in the nest so that she can keep them safe from enemies.

When they are two months old, Mum takes the cubs on their first outing to the big, open, African plains. She lets them follow her through the tall grass, where they can hide more easily from dangerous animals such as lions. Keeping up with their mum's big steps is hard work!

Sometimes a cheetah mum will perch high on a termite mound, so she can see above the long grass and watch out for other animals. When the cubs are older, she will teach them how to hunt for gazelles, rabbits and other food.

Cheetahs live in open grasslands, where the sun is very bright and it can get unbearably hot. The cubs keep cool in the middle of the day by lying under the shade of Mum's tummy.

But it's not always hot, and when it rains, the family gets soaking wet. Not to worry! Mum quickly licks her cubs clean and dry. Her tongue is like a washcloth and the cubs love their 'baths'!

Cheetah cubs are full of energy and love to play. They spend a lot of time playing with each other, but they also like to play with Mum. She lets them bite her tail and climb all over her. Other animals, like tortoises, sometimes get caught up in their games as well!

It's too dangerous for the cubs to follow Mum while she hunts, so she finds a safe place for them to hide – sometimes even under a tiny bush. They have to keep as quiet and still as possible, until Mum comes back.

Mum is out hunting and she has spotted a tasty gazelle. She starts to run really fast and chases the gazelle as it zig-zags to try and escape. She sticks her tail in the air to keep balance.

Mum has done a great job feeding her cubs. Now they are three months old, and they are much bigger and stronger. But they will stay with Mum until they are two years old. She still needs to teach them how to survive on the plains.

When the cubs are six months old, they play much more boisterous, big-cub games. The brothers and sisters love to chase, tackle and play-fight.

Even though they are playing very rough, they never hurt each other. This kind of play helps to make their muscles and bones grow strong.

When the cubs are nearly two years old they are as big as their mother. Mum has taught them everything they need to know to survive on their own. Now they can hunt for their own food. It is almost time for them to leave home and start their adult lives.

After all Mum's love, care and teaching, the cubs are able to look after themselves. They can catch their own food, find their own shelter, and protect themselves from danger. Best of all, they can now run as fast as the big cheetahs! One day, they will start a cheetah family of their own.

More about Cheetahs

- Cheetahs have hundreds of spots. These spots help to hide them in the tall grass where they hunt.

- The black lines under cheetahs' eyes (which look like tears) protect their eyes by reflecting the strong sun.

- Cheetahs chirp like birds! A cheetah's call sounds like a chirp. They also purr loudly when they are happy, and growl or hiss when they are scared.

- Cheetahs run faster than all other animals on land. At top speed, they can run nearly 100 kilometres or 60 miles per hour. That's as fast as a car on the motorway.

- While other cats hunt at night, cheetahs do most of their hunting during the day.

- Cheetahs can go without drinking water for 3 or 4 days.

- Cheetahs live in eastern, central and south-western Africa and a small portion of Iran. They are are endangered because people are destroying the grassy areas they live in and poaching the animals they hunt.

- Find out more on www.cheetah.org